I Do.... Or Do I?

Assistance To Becoming One

By

Devorias Jackson

CONTENTS

FOREWORD

Life has its ways of choosing the right individuals to tell lessons that produce phenomenal testimonies regardless of whether they feel worthy of the opportunity. It's been quite a ride to get to this point in my life. Through God's strength and guidance, I am ready to share a few life lessons hoping that it would truly help others. Throughout my experiences shared here, I would say that I was blessed with knowledge and practical wisdom that everyone can tap from and practice. It is the practical knowledge that, when acquired and practiced, will assist those who desire to be married, want to remain married, and even those of us who are divorced and want to be re-married. I hope that these lessons and practices would penetrate the hearts of those seeking to understand the concepts and revelations placed into the earth before it even was.

1

IN THE BEGINNING

Let's be completely honest and transparent for a minute. Relationships, let alone marriages, CAN BE TOUGH!!!! The task of becoming one with another individual with a completely different upbringing and viewpoint is hard enough, not to mention the endless compromising done to appease the union's peace. It takes a lot... But it's doable!

I had to go through a few things that I never thought I would go through to see the beauty of marriage. For the sake of experiences, I would give you a real-life example of what to do and not do. Many could disagree with me on this subject, as technically being married and divorced twice. Although they were not successful, I received some valuable wisdom and knowledge that ultimately ushered me to the feet of God. There, and only there was He able to reveal to me the true character of a mate.

Even as an adult man, I can hear my mother's voice repeating one of her familiar sayings, "Devorias, there's no testimony without the test." I hope you all would consider this book a study guide or cheat sheet to obtain a passing score to your test/testimony for those seeking a union. Now, I'll be sincere. I do not hold a certificate that states I hold a certification for courses to counsel pre-marital and married couples; I only hold life experiences that hold considerable creditability and recognition in the University of Real Life.

If you're expecting this book to go something like, "It all started in April, the 25th day of 1985; a little boy was born in the dawn of the morning to two loving adults," then you may need to go ahead and close this book now.

It's not one of those books, but since we are here, let me share a little insight into my beginnings. I think then you'd have a solid understanding of where my desire to want to be a spouse came from. For most, they receive the feeling later in life after many have worn out the lifestyle of singleness. For me, the moment I saw the joys of marriage, I knew that's where I was supposed to be. Interestingly enough, when I first opened a bible, one of the most profound things that I read was that God destined us (humankind) at the beginning of our existence to be with someone.

We see this in the book of Genesis 2:18, where God stated, "It is not good that the man should be alone; I will make him a helper suitable for him." While this scripture referred to Adam, who was the only man, we also see in the same book where it relates to a woman as a Helpmeet and that she came out of Man. This was the eccentric plan, which God had in mind for both sexes.

In today's time, we understand the life cycle order because a man's seed must impregnate a woman in some fashion or form to conceive a child. So at best, we can now conclude that without women, there could be no more men, and without men, there could be no more women.

This union has stemmed some of the greatest events in life, whether good or bad. Memories of pains, new experiences, births, and even deaths have been created through marriage. Amazingly everything but what God designed for marriages is now happening in today's marriages at an alarming rate. Christ commanded the husband to love his wife as He did the church and for the wife to submit herself unto her husband in respect. (See Ephesians 5:22-33 KJV)

I purposefully placed the husband's command first. In the Bible, the husband was commanded secondly. Now ask yourself this question, "If God placed Man here first, why then was man commanded to do such as an emotion that is needed for a union?" In my discovery and revelation, we must look at the generalization and importance of women first.

In Proverbs 8, the wisdom given to Solomon by God was personified as the gender of a female. Throughout these verses of scripture, Wisdom explains her origin and purpose. Verses like, "[22]The LORD possessed me in the beginning of his way, before his works of old. [23]I was set up from everlasting, from the beginning, or ever the earth was." And, "[30]Then I was by him, as one brought up with him: and I was daily his delight, rejoicing always before him; 31Rejoicing in the habitable part of his earth; and my delights were with the sons of men." (Proverbs 8:22-23; 30-31 KJV)

Showing this correlation of events presents the idea that while man's idea was in God's plan, so was the woman's from the beginning. In the make-up of His work, He found purposes for both. Man would be the protector (physical covering), provider (the worker), priest (spiritual advisor), and leader (head) of the home, and wife; well, she would be the wisdom (spiritual connection to God) behind the whole operation. I firmly believe that while man is first in the eyes of our Father, He knew that the woman would be a vital key in men's lives.

For instance, Moses loved his wife Zipporah, daughter of Jethro. However, in this union, Zipporah was not one of God's chosen people, "the Children of Israel." Moses married her anyway, and they conceived a son named Gershom.

Moses knew of his roots and knew there were certain laws he had to abide by in the upholding of God's chosen people. One of those things being circumcision, eight days after the male child was born. Moses, for whatever reason, did not follow this law, and for that, God sought to kill Moses. (See Exodus 4:24-26 KJV). He was saved only by his wife's acts, who circumcised her son, despite not being of the Hebrew heritage.

Now here's the proposed question that I found asking myself. "How did Zipporah know God was about to kill Moses?" and "How did she know what actions would save him?" The bible only speaks of cause and effect in this story, but some of us can speculate that Zipporah had some type of relationship with God, that He, Himself communicated to her that He would kill Moses unless this was done.

Amazing, isn't it? That God used an unorthodox method to bring back orthodox order. So why do we feel that marriage is so hard? Why do we persist in listening to others explain to us the Do's and the Don'ts, yet we still struggle independently? One reason is that we truly don't understand the significance and meaning of marriage. The second reason is that we refuse to believe that it actually can be an easier process, and three, do we truly desire to do it God's way to reap the true benefits and joy of matrimony?

Through the practice of these various phases in this book, I believe that you will either find the one God has destined for you or be able to keep and better that one that God has already given you. Get ready to embark on the part of the abundant life that God intended us to have!

2

CHOOSING AND COURTING VS. SETTLING AND DATING

I'm sure by now you're wondering what mystery plan or secret I have discovered, so profound to be worthy of concluding that it will lead to marital bliss. I would have to shockingly surprise you by saying, nothing out of the ordinary. It is nothing simpler than an ear to hear, a heart to comprehend, and a willingness to apply God's word to my life.

Have you ever wondered what dating really was and where it came from? The word "date" can be traced back to the 1800s Medieval Latin, where the origins of the word "dare" or "to give" came from. As time passed, the word took significance in the Latin language, on into French dialect "data" or "to deliver." These words may not seem in any way relatable, although their correlation reached today's definition, which means, "To go out with (someone in whom one is romantically or sexually interested)."

Let's see if I got this right; I dared myself or gave reason enough to want to share data or deliver information to let you know I was romantically or sexually interested....? Funny enough, this is the idea of the world. We seek mates and feel the need to allow our attraction to lay claim to an individual or individuals we know nothing about but place ourselves there based on the idea of romance and human sexuality.

This works for some, but others find themselves chasing emptiness. After the smoke has cleared, still desiring a nonexistent fill-up and craving the damsel's happy ending in distress, or prince charming coming to save the day. What is then associated with these feelings is the urgency to settle down. Settling is linked to more divorces and bad relationships than natural causes.

Most feel it years into their marriages that they have fallen out of love or are no longer being fulfilled in the way they once were before. Before the work, maybe kids, or just plain life, many find that their marriages' success seems no longer in reach. However, consequently having these feelings births affairs, secret lives, and destruction of the family unit.

The Bible states, "What therefore God hath joined together, let no man put asunder." (Mark 10:9 KJV) That means no man, including you!! Why is this so profound? It is so profound because "self" can be the biggest enmity to any life choice or decision we make in life, especially in choosing mates. We sometimes make simple hasty and wrong choices due to our flesh's lust. Whatever the reason, those choices stem guilt and resentment.

Dating doesn't prove much of anything except your ability to be attracted to another individual. Yea, you've asked questions to get to know the person, but nine times out of ten, a person's identity doesn't surface until about a month or two. In most cases, you find out that they are not who you believe them to be, leaving you feeling like it has been time wasted, the time you could have spent on the person you truly desired. The act of courting, if done properly, can alleviate the pain of wasted time when it comes to choosing a spouse. You see, courting does not strain you in any way.

You may have just looked at that reference to courting, and now you're asking yourself, "isn't dating and courting the same thing?"

Yes....and definitely no.

I say this confidently by studying this matter, and I'll show you. Let's go back to the Webster's Dictionary and look at society's dating definition. "To go out with someone in whom one is romantically or sexually interested in." Now, here's the definition for courting: to be involved with romantically, typically with the intention of marrying. You see, romance is fine; without it, I don't think you can truly love an individual you say you want to be with, but the biggest thing about it is the intention and path of the romance. If we were to survey 100 people of what they think, we would probably discover that many would say dating typically leads to sex, and courting implies marriage.

Courting allows you the true option of choice, not so much by yourself but with God. While courting, your standards are raised higher. You can choose guidelines and regulations. The do's, the don'ts, the can's, and the will not's are very apparent.

In so many ways, you uphold the standards of God in keeping yourself holy and allowing yourself time and space to get to know the individual you are courting. Men, this is huge for us! Why? Because men are visual beings, we normally go after it without regard when we like what we see. Consider this technique to examine the fruit and keep yourself in a place to understand it before actually taking and consuming it. This takes prayer, patience, and self-control, all attributes of a true man of God or one following after God's heart.

Ladies, I did not forget about you. This gives you the ability to see a man's true intentions, moreover, his mannerisms, conversations, mentalities, but most importantly, his direction. If he's not willing to be patient with you and God, then he isn't worthy to have you and God. You see how I included God there as a pair. That's because a man should find you through seeking God first. There should never be any other way.

So you got the courting thing down, and decided that you want to be with this person, what's next...? Prayer and fasting, of course! What gets us in trouble most times is our wants, normally that of our flesh's lust, but we always want God's will for our lives and whom He wants us to be aligned with in His will. This should make you want what God wants for you spiritually more than what you desire naturally.

We can receive this by spending time with God and staying before His presence, especially considering our mates.

Later in this book, you will find out that praying for your spouse is the glue in keeping your marriage together. Why not start initially, even before the wedding, vows, and hopefully much later, children. This place is where you find out what God has to say about your courting matters. Simply asking God to show you if this person is right for you in His will gives God full authority to show you things about the individual that He either does or doesn't approve of.

This is the kicker; though God says no, listen to Him! And because you guys chose to court instead of to date, a lot of the time it's easier to say, "Hey, I really enjoyed spending time with you, but I believe friendship is all I can really afford to offer." To some, those can be the hardest words to hear but imagine if you didn't heed God's voice and continued with it. Those are problems you don't want. Words to the wise…. when God says no, listen!

So if you don't remember much, remember that dating looks at romance through more physical attraction, and courting allows you to focus on romance through God.

3

VOWS, COMMITMENT, AND COVENANT

If you ever heard of Abraham's story, you would remember that one of the most profound things was God's promises to him. Often, we tend to forget that God has not forgotten His own Vows, commitment, and covenant made with Abraham. The Bible states, "God is not a man, that he should lie; neither the son of man, that he should repent: hath he said, and shall he not do it? or hath he spoken, and shall he not make it good? (Numbers 23:19 KJV) while I understand that we are not God, we often tend to break vows, commitments, and covenants daily; moreover, the structured model has been set for us.

In the agreement of marriage or becoming married, we must understand that it begins with the idea and actual actions of doing it, more than just speaking about it. I'm sure many of us didn't just wake up and get married or decided we would be married but spoke the idea aloud. I know I did! I can recall the time, if not many, of times telling myself, and even other people, "I desire or want to be married." It's funny how quick those words are said and how slow the union's actions progress.

I want you to focus on the most redundant cliche that is often said unconsciously, "usually, what you speak is what you get." This can be associated with the Laws of Attractions for some and others karma. However, the scripture states, "Death and life are in the power of the tongue: and they that love it shall eat the fruit thereof." (Proverbs 18:21 KJV) Now let me break this down for some of you who don't realize or know...WATCH YOUR MOUTH!!!

I chuckled as I wrote that, only because I know it all too well. Even funnier and most interesting is the fact that God knew as well. He made the world, and all that is in it, by His thoughts and words alone. Since we have been made in His image, and after His likeness, furthermore, how much more proof do we need to know that we possess the same ability. I said that choosing a mate or being with your spouse in the marriage is about saying the right things because of the power that words possess. The trio of promises' significance; Vows, commitment, and covenant is the basis of promises made on three different levels. I will explain.

It starts at the beginning, but at the lowest level of promise being the "Vow…." Let's look at the word "Vow," in the Merriam-Webster dictionary, "a serious promise to do something or to behave in a certain way." This is normally the promise made in front of people at the wedding. The maid of honor and the best man are usually the closest to the bride and groom. Their purpose, along with the audience and participants in the wedding, is to hear the husband-to-be and wife-to-be's' vows. This, therefore, helps in keeping the memory of what is said by the two.

They are the ones who should remind the husband and wife of the promises or vows they made, which is to "behave in a certain way" to their spouses to uphold the values of the marriage. This should be an indicator to many deciding to be married to pick someone mature who can tell you the truth when it comes down to those moments when you contemplate separating or even when you get out of line as a wife or husband.

For those who are married now or sometime soon, I would suggest you call your best man or maid of honor and ask them if they remember your vows. If they don't, talk it out with them about what vow you desire them to remind you of so that if you ever found yourself in a place of a needed reminder, it would be no problem to state in love. This is truly important because normally, people will listen to the counsel of a close friend who they know is honest before they listen to others.

The second level of promise is "commitment"! Again, Merriam-Webster defines it as such "A promise to do or give something; to be loyal to someone or something; the attitude of someone who works very hard to do or support something. Isn't it exciting how this sounds familiar for those of us who are married or have been married? Those of you either seeking to be married or are engaged, listen up!

The minister of the ceremony normally gives you a list of questions to answer with the phrase, "I Do." Do you take this woman or man...? In sickness and in health...? For richer or poorer...? For Better or for worst...? Till death do you part...?

This is where you've said or are going to say...

WAIT! Hold on, just one moment. Before you say the conclusion answer to these commitments, let's briefly view them in another way to show their true importance.

First, do you take this man or woman? Meaning, do you exactly take what you see before you? This man or woman standing in front of you, not a person of potentials, or what you're wishing would or could be, but more importantly, this man or woman who you have chosen.

Sometimes we pray and pray for a person to change, not really understanding that the person you decided to marry or have married is the person they are. Nothing changes about them but the days, but you chose them despite knowing or not allowing enough time to get to know this because you figured they would change, or you could change them. Let me tell you a small secret if no one has ever told you; God is the only one that can change anyone.

Secondly, through the flaws, life changes, difficult and exciting times, do you commit to being there for this man or woman? Today, individuals jump ship at the slightest shift in their relationships. Amazingly, we fail to realize that God is God, and even He understands the times would and will change. Ecclesiastes 3:1-8 gives examples of what is to be expected in this life, and for some odd reasons, many believe they are exempt from this rule.

This information isn't to deter you from making these outstanding commitments or even scare the ones who are currently married; it's only subtle advice to prepare you or gear you toward the road ahead. One of my favorite scriptures in the bible commands that we, "Trust in the LORD with all your heart; and lean not unto your own understanding. In all your ways acknowledge him, and he shall direct your paths." (Proverbs 3:5-6 KJV)

This assures us that while God understands that tests and trials will come in His people's lives, He will show us how to go so that those times will not be as bad as imagined. He never said the weapons would not come; He just promised that they would not prosper.

Lastly, Till Death' do us part... This is self-explanatory...Right? Yet, many do not believe in this anymore due to our lust. I'm not telling you not to get married or even stay married if abuse or blatant infidelity is going on, but what I am saying is that God is a Mender, a Healer, and a Heart Changer!

He can do things that no counselor or even a pastor could do in the hearts of spouses, but it takes your faith, your will to fight, and sacrifice. Some have given only a part of their time and effort to save their marriages. Ask yourself this question, if that man or woman is supposed to be a part of you, would you give up on yourself? Most would answer no, yet we give up so easily on others that we call "spouses."

Commitment takes more determination than it does work. You need a strong mind to say, I do, or I will, and an attitude to back up the actions. Commitment is directed toward the person in the mirror. Can you commit yourself to yourself? If you can, you are ready to proceed to the next and most important level of the promises: the covenant!

Now that you had stated your vows before your family and friends and either committed or re-committed yourself to your spouse, next must come the spiritual unifying of the promises.

A covenant is a binding contract or promise made to and between God by you and your spouse. We can see many times where God made covenants with His children and even people who helped out His children along the way. This is important to remember because again, God states, "He is not a man, that should neither lie, nor the son of man that He would have to repent." (Numbers 23:19 KJV)

This alone is a bold statement of God to tell us that while we may break a binding promise or covenant, He will not. It is so serious that every place where God made a covenant, He sealed it with a blood sacrifice. Abraham's promise was sealed with the ram in the bush instead of his son's life; moreover, as we know, God had asked him to sacrifice his only son. The sins committed by His children of Israel were pardoned through various animals and grain sacrifices. And even the ultimate sacrifice was God shedding the blood of His only son for the promise of redemption and everlasting life for you and me, who choose to accept His son into our lives as our savior.

He has even found a way to seal the covenant of marriage, binding us through blood. Without being totally graphic, I'll briefly explain.

When a woman has reached a mature age, she develops a "Hymen." The hymen is a thin, fleshy tissue that is stretched across part of the opening of the vagina. When a man and woman have sexual intercourse for the first time, this hymen is broken by the man entering the woman, causing a small amount of blood to bleed out.

This is the binding seal on the covenant that is made by God. However, we live in a society where sex has been taken leisurely, and intended purpose has been devalued. Casual sex, a friend with benefits, and all forms of pre-marital sex have become the norm. So, what is the binding seal to the individuals who aren't virgins themselves when they get married……? It's still the act of sex, of course! This is still a pivotal part of God's covenant because sex was originally and purposefully given to the married couple as a gift.

It was… and is designed for them. Through sexual intercourse comes the attaching of souls. This is called a "soul-tie" because two souls intermingle by entering one another's body. A man deposits not only his seed or semen, but his character, personality, and spirit into a woman, and in turn, a woman receives it into her own body; consequently, a transfer of her spirit, character, and personality back into the man as a reoccurring model.

Therefore, it's important to make sure that those desiring to be married, who have had sex before, seek God and ask for repentance. We should seek God for the complete deliverance from any individuals we may still be tied to in the spirit because of pre-marital sex. This prevents you from bringing it to your soon-to-be spouse and even bringing those spirits into your home. This may require extensive prayer and fasting, but it is worth it; you owe it to yourself and soon to be spouse.

For those who are already married, this may be a great time to examine yourself and see if you have allowed other spirits to enter your bedroom and even between your covenant with God. It's never too late to search and correct that which may hold you back from the marriage God intended you and your spouse to have. Seek help from your pastor for spiritual advice, and even sit down with your spouse after praying about what to say, and talk with your spouse about things that you feel are preventing you from being the best husband or wife you could be.

In the book of Genesis 2:25, it states, "And they were both naked, the man and his wife, and were not ashamed." Many interpret this scripture to mean naked in a physical sense, but you must realize that they did not know they were naked until after consuming the fruit from the tree. What is meant when it is said they were "naked" and "unashamed?" We can conclude that they had no secrets, concluding nothing was hidden from one another. Secrets are the silent killers of many relationships or marriages. Don't allow secrets to hinder the power of your vow, commitment, and covenant made toward marriage.

4

THE HONEYMOON

What can be said…? As many of you can imagine or even envision, the honeymoon is one of the biggest thrills, and most looked forward to the marriage union's event. Most times, married couples and even couples to-be will have already imagined and planned out in their minds this fantasy-filled experience, or even plans for the 2nd and 3rd honeymoon.

The idea behind the honeymoon experience is positioned in the marriage's physical and sensual part. This is where both husband and wife can explore themselves intimately through physical desires and spiritual connection through their spouses for however long the honeymoon lasts. However, the honeymoon should not be timed or even appointed for a mere matter of days but should be practiced and experienced continuously throughout the marriage.

We should make all honeymoons until the moon rises no more! Meaning we should be honeymooning until we die! This section is most vital because it is taken too likely a lot of times. Consummation or sex was a gift that God Himself designed and gave to the married man and married woman of the same union. The bible shows where God has given one of His first commandments to man and woman. It states that He (God) blessed them, and God said unto them, "Be fruitful, and multiply, and replenish the earth, and subdue it: and have dominion over the fish of the sea, and over the fowl of the air, and over every living thing that moveth upon the earth." (Genesis 1:28 KJV)

The whole idea was simple and plain. God had created the earth, the skies, and the water, placed the ground in the middle, planted vegetation, and placed animals there; concluding these things, He then gave it to man. Once a man had a hold of it, worked it, and educated himself of this world, God blessed him with the woman and the ability to procreate life with her. Now, while I know most of you are reading, saying…but "I'm not ready for children!" I completely understand; I truly only stated this to show the primary reasoning behind sex, and not only just for pleasure alone. For the sake of time, we will quickly look at the areas of God's gift in the idea and plan for it through intimacy.

When you consider intimacy, most times than naught, the first thing that comes to mind in its majority is the physicality of the act of intimacy. This can be defined as touching, kissing, holding, etc. However, intimacy is defined as "close familiarity or friendship; closeness." I truly enjoy reading some of the synonyms listed for "intimacy," words like rapport, confidence, amity, and togetherness.

It is remarkable how sexual relations or sexual intercourse is the last definition to describe intimacy. We can conclude this because sexual intercourse or relations is one of the easiest things to do. Anyone or everyone is capable of this action from birth. No one is taught how, but we understand the actions and nature. Yet, it is often one of the first things we analyze when considering becoming intimate with someone.

I have this speculation that what leads to this world- like perverted thinking is our flesh and the earnestness to feed it through lust. God explains in so many ways that we are born into sin, even though we can resist it through the death of His son Jesus. Paul went on further to explain himself in this scripture, stating, "**18** And I know that nothing good lives in me, that is, in my sinful nature.[a] I want to do what is right, but I can't. **19** I want to do what is good, but I don't. I don't want to do what is wrong, but I do it anyway" (Romans 7:18-19 NLT)

This is just to show our sinful nature, naturally wanting what the flesh desires when it comes to intimacy without God's will in mind. The flesh is what we struggle to tame the most regarding courting, dating, and even sometimes in marriage. Some may disagree and quote the scripture that states, "Marriage is honorable in all, and the bed undefiled: but whoremongers and adulterers God will judge." (Hebrew 13:4 KJV) Many who are married or about to marry love this scripture; in their misunderstanding, they believe it gives them a pass to do whatever they desire with their marriage.

While I will say this scripture does authorize freedom when married; furthermore, if not careful, we can find ourselves still in the wrong with the same scripture due to overlooking wordage. Let's examine this scripture briefly. First, "Marriage is honorable in all," this is stating the obvious: God sanctions marriage, putting His stamp of approval on it. Secondly, "and the bedroom is undefiled, but whoremongers and adulterers God will judge."

Why would God warn us right after saying that "marriage is honorable in all"? Let's go back and look at the word intimacy, or Into-Me-I-See. This breaks it down better to understand just how private the matters are of the bedroom or any marriage intimacy. Only you and your spouse should know what goes on in this space. Whoremongers and adulterers are not born; they are created. How, you ask...? From the lust of their own flesh, births sin.

What goes into our ears and eyes leads to our mind, fed to our hearts, and from the heart comes out in our actions. "Keep your heart with all diligence,

For out of it spring the issues of life." (Proverbs 4:23 KJV) "The heart is deceitful above all things, and desperately wicked: who can know it?" (Jeremiah 17:9 KJV) These are just a few examples expounding on what happens when things become rooted in our hearts.

Ladies, unfortunately, by you sharing what you believe to be harmless banter with your girlfriends what goes down in the bedroom or with your husband intimately, in little words or less, you are defiling your bed space. Guys, you didn't think I forgot about you... did you? Sometimes as men, we feel the need to boast and brag to our guy friends to show a sense of pride and authority. We pride ourselves, especially when it comes to our spouses, in showing "who's the man of the house" due to our conquering nature. However, it's defiling God's gift to us in being intimate with our own assigned spouses.

It may seem harmless, and you may say I trust my friend, but I'm simply enlightening you that you create thoughts that enter into people's minds about your spouses. This could be by illustrating the things they do for you. These are ways that whoremongers and adulterers are created; because we never know what transpires in someone's mind after leaving our presence. I was always told that all it takes is the right place, the right timing, and the right feeling to make a mistake of a lifetime.

The easiest way to fix these issues is to keep what gift God has granted our spouse and us, this intimate freedom, to the confines of our minds. I know problems sometimes arise requiring a solution about sexuality in your marriage but seek professional help, and if professional help doesn't alleviate the circumstance, take it to God. He does always remind us that NOTHING is IMPOSSIBLE for Him! YES! Nothing!!

While this is one of the primary ways to interrupt God's blessings through intimacy, a huge hindrance in marriages is soul ties. I have heard Christian couples, married and engaged to be, speak on some of the nastiest things when it comes to sex, in the belief again that the "Bedroom being undefiled to the married couple" gives them all freedom. I asked myself, where did these ideas come from? Who started this fallacy that anything and everything was a green light just because you were married?

Often, where we destroy a good thing, is bringing outside influences from our past. Listen, I get that the scripture says the bedroom is undefiled, but only for those two in that designated arraignment. Yes, just between those two! This means that what is done in your past relationship or past lifestyle needs to be emptied of mind. Moreover, the thoughts of things done with others should be erased. The acts of intimacy in your married bedroom should be directed toward what you and your spouse enjoy together. The focus should be becoming One Flesh with your spouse and not seeking what you are accustomed to, or even what you've done to someone before you believe your spouse will enjoy.

This is completely wrong, and honestly, you turn into that whoremonger and that adulterer because you have brought what was done to another soul into your intimate space, causing a type of "spiritual orgy." Disgusting as it may sound, we tend to do it all the time without even knowing we are due to us wanting to please our spouses.

Therefore, it is crucial to eliminate soul ties and being intimate before consummation and before moving forward with the idea of marriage. I'll tell you, along with many others in the body of Christ that some soul ties are stronger than others, and some are deeply rooted. This is especially true for those who have either forfeited their virginity to individuals before marriages. It is also true with those who have spent a prolonged time in relationships with pre-marital sex as the norm. However, like Jesus explained to the disciple who could not route out the evil spirit in the man vexed with demonic presences' legions. "This kind can come forth by nothing, but by prayer and fasting." (Mark 9:29 KJV)

The honeymoon is the most prolific time of the marriage, and again should be practiced every day. Honeymoon includes being intimate or creating closeness bonds through talks, prayer, bible study, and yes, sex. This helps to build the bond that God intended for the married man and woman to have through His gifting.

5

FOR BETTER, AND DEFINITELY FOR WORSE

Imagine going into a car lot and walking around looking for the car of your dreams. As you search and search, you find yourself anxious and somewhat frustrated that the vehicle has not yet been found. You have test-driven multiple styles and various makes, but you can't seem to find the one you want. Out of the corner of your eye, you see it! The car you feel is the one and you tell the dealer that you have made up your mind to take the red one!

Unfortunately, you failed to realize that the car, while it is for sale, it's in the mechanical service area. The dealer warns you and tries to show you better models of cars you desire, but you have fallen in love, and no one can change your mind. Along the line, the dealer and the finance manager even gave the Carfax reports, showing that it has been in several wrecks, has maintenance issues, and minor work that is still needed. This was the main reason why it wasn't on the sales lot.

You sign the papers anyway, collect the keys, and roll off into the sunset. Music blasting, all windows completely down; you show the world your beautiful metal masterpiece. Several weeks go by, and you're still in shock of having what you believe to be the car of your dreams, as it shows in your eyes. Suddenly, the vehicle's check engine light illuminates and turns off. You pay it no mind because this is your vehicle that you take pride in and love. You go as far as repeatedly reminding everyone that this is your blessing from God.

Months pass, and you smell smoke, and you realize something isn't right. You take it in for service, and they begin to tell you that some slight issues need repair. They go on to tell you that these are things that should have been taken care of months, if not years ago. After much money spent on repairs, your morale and love have decreased. You start to notice things about the car you dislike and even hate. You now find yourself contemplating selling or trading this once wonderful art of a vehicle. One problem, you have made a contractual agreement with the bank binding you to agreements of terms, even though you ignored all the red flags before purchasing it. If you break this agreement, you could be penalized more than purchasing this vehicle.

The question now is, "Do I keep it and continue to put more money and work into it to restore it to its once magnificent state" or "Do I count it as loss and take my chances with the penalties?" The decision becomes harder and harder as time goes on. Some days are better than most and you feel dumb for ever buying this car on other days.

This story sounds so familiar for some of us, doesn't it? This may be an experience you had buying your first vehicle, but the familiarity I'm referring to is those of us, especially married or divorced. This is what marriage can feel and has felt like at the beginning and the end. I really want you to pay close attention to this part because it could save you so much burden and time. The key to understanding this issue in marriage is that our expectations of the individuals we love will look blurry at some point.

Your answer should resonate loudly in your thoughts as you hear the officiator asks the most infamous question of any wedding in front of friends and family. But sometimes, because we expect to be asked something that's been done and heard over and over, we don't give it a second thought. Do you take this woman or man to have, for better or worse? Wait a minute! Can you repeat that Mr minister? I mean, I know I take her or him for the better; but what do you mean for the worse? Many have pondered this question in their heads in the waiting rooms, altars, living and bedrooms, and even family functions.

What really makes this such a huge pill to swallow? Maybe because we associate it with only the good memories and none of the bad when we think of marriage. I mean, who thinks about marrying someone for all the bad things to happen? I know I didn't! But the reality is we live in a world with sin surrounding us at every possible angle. The enemy hates the institution and the establishment of marriage because of the power that comes from it. "Two are better than one; because they have a good reward for their labor." (Ecclesiastes 4:9 KJV) Did you catch that? This scripture is a confirmation that two is not only better than one, but when they work together, they receive a good reward.

I believe that many forget this marriage aspect in the hindsight of things. It is work, but the work done for the Father in Heaven matters the most. Love is the answer; love in a relationship, i.e., marriages, is a super plus because honestly, without it, there could be no effective result for the marriage union. However, we have to get to a place where love does not catch us off guard from life's realities.

The connection between my story of purchasing a car and marriage shows what many who call themselves lovers go through. They go through this right before and on into the married life. We may meet as individuals and fall madly in love, often looking past the flaws and the warnings, even those warnings from others looking at us from another perspective. Consequently, we got married, honeymoon, then build a home, just to find out there are things that have always been there; things that literally annoy the heck out of you, or some things we can't live with.

At times, this has made many reevaluate the whole marriage, wondering did they honestly make the right decision. When I first wrote the book, I was almost led to name this chapter "the beer belly and ugly feet phase." This illustrates that we know ugly feet and beer bellies don't just appear; they in some instances were either already there or will eventually come; however, we chose to overlook them at the beginning due to being so blinded in love and other times it gets harder to overlook while you're deep into the marriage..

So, to be upset that you're starting to notice or focus on it must show you the type of attack that the enemy chooses to play in your mind. The mind is a battlefield, and we are the infantry on the field. However, we have a God, as Solomon stated in Proverbs 18:10, "The name of the Lord is a strong tower: the righteous runneth into it and are safe."

I said this to say that we must find ourselves with the same love we started with, in the "better" times, even on into "worse" times. This was explained to me by illustrating "watering the grass to choke out the weed." What was furthermore explained to me is that this technique has saved countless lawn care enthusiasts from losing their pride and joy.

I know it's probably difficult to follow where I'm going with this, but for clarity, this is explained: When a weed grows around, and amongst the grass, you find it most difficult to find a solution to figure out how to get rid of them. Some would say pull it, and while you absolutely could, you risk pulling out patches of grass that the weed's roots have connected to. Some others would say use a weed killer; even with that solution, the chemicals meant to kill the weed most time inadvertently kill the grass and defeat the purpose.

How do you rid the weeds, then?

Can you believe that you can kill the weeds by strategically feeding the grass? By using a method called "aerating." Normally, this requires some machine or tool that places small holes in the ground, allowing air and much-needed nutrients to penetrate the soil. After the process, normally, the gardener will overseed and fertilized the holey ground and then proceed to water profusely.

You may be asking, what exactly in the world does this have to do with the issues and flaws I see in my mate? This is the same method we must use to kill our marriages' negativity. Let's look at this from a spiritual perspective. We must use the tool called love to poke small holes in our spouses. After this, we use wisdom and the words of love to overseed and fertilize this holy ground.

Men and women are so much alike in many ways. We both enjoy compliments and praise, and we detest annoyance and criticism. So, use words of love to uplift instead of tear down. Instead of telling someone how much they get on your nerves, try telling them how much you love them and how much they mean to you; even more, how you noticed the awesome job they've done on cooking dinner or how they cleaned out the car.

From a man's perspective, I can only speak here, but if a spouse told me a few lovely things about how well I've done, you could bet that more of that will get done in the future because words of love give life and not death. We understand this because the word of God backs this by stating, "Death and life are in the power of the tongue: and they that love it shall eat the fruit thereof." (Proverbs 18:21 KJV)

The watering or the praying is the final step in building your spouse's character. As I told you earlier in this book, prayers are necessary for your spouse. Prayer is speaking to the Father about our concerns out of our own abilities. It is a way to stay rooted, conscious of the mission of marriage, and protect us, our marriage, and ultimately our families, from the wiles of the enemy. Satan would have you forget to pray for your spouse because it gives him the advantage to attack secretly and undetected. Normally, when you notice an attack on your spouse or marriage, it is too late.

Prayers for your spouse not only protect but cover future attacks that the enemy plans. Watering implies the continuous motion of placing water on something. So, just as you would water your grass to allow it to grow and choke out the weeds. Use Love, your words, and continuous prayers to look past your spouse's flaws or soon-to-be. Above all, let's make sure we're growing and nurturing those good things that you do love and cherish.

6

ACCEPTANCE

To be truly accepted in life, I would have to express that marriage is one of the best feelings in this lifetime. Confidence is what drives us from one achievement to the other. When we lack confidence or faith in ourselves, we find that the outcome is usually the formation of a rut or excuse that follows. This is a killer and prevention to progression. It is the same not only in life but in marriage. Men and women often look to their spouses for validation, and many of the time become sorely disappointed by what they feel is the lack of.

This validation is expected; however, true validation comes from above and within. It is a lesson that should be quickly learned going into a marriage and also in the maintaining of one. We believe that strength is drawn from inside oneself, or one's ability; but, I have a question. What happens when the man or woman in the mirror no longer fits the husband or wife's image you have always desired to be?

I have had this happen many times to me; for example, I would come home from a long day at work tired only to realize it was time to clock in another job (Marriage Inc.). My wife at the time cared not to understand how my day went. She did only know that initially something in the house was not working properly and needed immediate attention.

I honestly could have cared less about the shower door or the bottom of the bed needing more support at this very time. My only question as a man I needed an answer to was, "can you still take a shower?" and "is the bed still sleep capable?" This is usually a typical man's response. However, what stuck out to me in the situation most wasn't the bed or the shower. It was a sign of aggravation from my spouse's face due to my inattentive attitude.

I hadn't shown any enthusiasm or concern toward what was important to my spouse, and for that, I unaware to myself, made my spouse feel unaccepted or inadequate. As busy individuals of life's grand scheme of things, we can and will do this more times than naught. This is complete unacceptance on so many levels. No matter how much work we have, how many meetings are called, and how important some things may mean to you. Your spouse is more important!

The natural order of life would suggest that you would place God at the highest platform, your children next, and lastly, your spouse. However, in the instructions of God, He desires that you place Him first, your spouse next, and a little after your children. I was taught by a pastor friend, that anything and everything else comes after that umbrella.

Why this order, you may be concerned? Well, because we see that in Genesis, that the foundation was slated as such. There was God, Adam then Eve, then Cain and Abel. Looking at these times that we live in, the kids often come before the acceptance of the spouse. This could be either because of the pandemic of adults marrying children out of wedlock or the emphasis on safeguarding the family's lineage.

Whatever the reason, when put into the formation or formula of a marriage, it is completely backwards. The seed could not be without a seed bearer. So why would you place the seed before the giver of the seed? While I take no importance away from the seed; moreover, your direction should be to take care of the bearer of seed, because the results in the production of good and plentiful seed are that the seed will ultimately one day grow, and either bare its own seed themselves or nurture the seed.

In Layman's terms, this means that the husband and wife normally pride themselves on creating a child or a family. While most succeed, the child or children grow, but naturally, at some age of maturity, they leave home to embark on ventures of their own lives, leaving the wife with her husband or the husband with his wife. If the order is ever scrambled to this is called neglecting the spouse. Through neglect, many spouses in marriages lose their sense of acceptance. This causes most separations to either happen or the beginning of consideration.

God's intentions were for man to take care of his own wife and for wives to take care of their own husbands. In Ephesians 5:28-29, "$_{28}$ So ought men to love their wives as their own bodies. He that loveth his wife loveth himself. $_{29}$ For no man ever yet hated his own flesh; but nourisheth and cherisheth it, even as the Lord the church." This precept shows the great example to men in their charge to love their wives by accepting them as their own bodies.

Let's jump back up to the precept right before this for the wife. We see that it states, "$_{21}$Submitting yourselves one to another in the fear of God. $_{22}$ Wives, submit yourselves unto your own husbands, as unto the Lord" (Ephesians 5:21-22 KJV) Now, isn't it ironic that the explanation of submission is directed to God, and then instructed for a wife to do this to her husband as unto the Lord?

This isn't meant to show partiality and never say that wives should be slaves to their husbands. Moreover, we remember that God spoke to Himself, His Son, and wisdom (woman), saying, "Let us make man in our image, and after our likeness…" (Genesis 1:26 KJV) Well, we understand now that we not only look like God, but we have a bit of His ability as well. What am I saying? I'm just conveying that when a wife can submit wholeheartedly to her godly husband in the flesh, it is nothing for her to submit to her true and living God in the spirit.

For these reasons, we can see the importance that God placed on acceptance, and why it is such an important marriage aspect. Remember that the things that we do in our marriage are in God's honoring and never a man. True validation is what you ultimately look like or reflect on God when you look in the mirror.

7

WHOLENESS

When you think about wholeness, how do you visualize it? What attributes or characteristics are associated with being whole? For many, the word that immediately comes to mind is "complete"! Completeness sets the standard that everything is either put together or is in its specific place and design. There usually is nothing missing, and if something does seem missing, it may not even be required or needed.

This is the perfect metaphor for marital wholeness in God's design and will; moreover, nothing is missing with God, and everything that is needed is given or will be received in due time. Many more times than often, couples who have embarked on the journey of marriage still seek things to make their marriage complete. The majority of the time, their marriages are in the perfected place of God. God asks simply four things, to be the center focus point, that we keep His commandments and love one another, and finally that He gets the glory in its entirety.

Yet, we as imperfect beings always seek perfection in places other than God Himself. This will cause major issues if not realized and ultimately corrected. We must understand that to reach that "perfection," it must line up to God's standards instead of our own or man's. Man's standards tell you that perfection or wholeness looks like the white picket fence, red-bricked single or double leveled home, with the tire swing in the front tree.

However, through the standards associated with our God, you'll recognize that there is a promise. Promise resulting of things, therefore intangible and protection from forces that would tear everything is man's standard into a pile of scraps as if an F-5 tornado hit it.

Godly wholeness first starts in the two separate individuals' hearts, seeking God's heart before marriage. This is normally either in the single-stage or during the courting stages that lead to marriage. Why is that? While God created us to be dependent on Him and later on one another; moreover, God also taught us first independence, in the learning of our purpose and design, and exactly who we are in Him, a.k.a. "self-love." Adam was given the garden and the animals to tend to (A job). God then allowed Adam to name the animals, and he waited for God's approval (An education). God, therefore, taught Adam the different precepts and rules of living and how to make Him happy ultimately through his commands (Religion and Relationship)

The whole while this was going on, Eve was in the heavens spending time with God learning her own purpose and design and what vital role she would play in Adam's life. She would be taught by the best teacher about patience, wisdom, submission, and love. She fellowshipped with God, and in turn, God trusted her enough to be wife to a husband. "[30] Then I was by him, as one brought up with him: and I was daily his delight, rejoicing always before him; [31] Rejoicing in the habitable part of his earth; and my delights were with the sons of men." (Proverbs 8:30)

In understanding marriage's eccentric design, you will find that the actual word marriage means wholeness or a completed union. Two flesh becoming one was not just a cliché or catchy phrase; it is verbiage that God knew would give power to the couple. We have all experienced a time or two in our lives in which we had to do a two-person job by ourselves. You may have been strong and talented enough to do so, especially these particular activities by yourself. Nonetheless, deep down, you knew if there was someone to share the load, it would be even easier than just doing it all by yourself.

This is the reason why God, in His infinite knowledge, knows that the union was necessary. He understood and still understands the wiles and troubles of this world. I could imagine He knew that even though He created man in the garden by Himself, man would eventually seek help from something or someone in the environment he was in. It was probably there, in that thought, where God's design in the architecture of humankind to look like Him caused a connection to the attraction of a man to a woman. Since then, when a man looked at a woman, and a woman looked at a man, consequently, no doubt would be formed, and that they would never forget that they were looking at God Himself.

The major issue in wholeness is the misconception that anything but God makes us whole through marriage. This is a trick of the enemy and even the mind since the beginning. We can understand this in the lives of Israel's children after leaving Egypt. God freed His people from the bondage that they had experienced 400 years. Through the miracles of a leader (Moses), plagues, and ultimately performed miracles before and during the trek through the wilderness, they still allowed themselves to have a void that they attempted to fill with everything but God.

This is a similar issue that plagues relationships and marriages today, believing that marriage can fill our voids and or even an individual. While marriage is superb and exciting, we must realize that we will not find that marital wholeness within marriage without being whole ourselves before marriage. It takes a conscious effort to really understand who you are and who you are in God.

God is referred to many times throughout the bible as a "Husbandmen." This title will help us understand how we can be whole before adding to someone or becoming an addition ourselves. "[22]Whoso findeth a wife findeth a good thing, and obtaineth favour of the LORD." (Proverbs 18:22) I have spoken on this particular passage many times and have even repeated it to myself as a reminder. I desired the favor from the Lord as a man of God. However, I overlooked something until recently in my previous search for a wife.

While very blatant and visible, I had never noticed the "Whoso findeth a *wife*" part. Before you ask whether I wear glasses or honestly read the bible, understand that we often rush over the meanings of the simplest words many times in our excitement. This particular scripture refers to the person finding not a girlfriend, soulmate, companion, etc. It says, wife!

This helps me bring my full understanding of the term husbandman, which was given to our Lord that I had explained earlier. You see, God is our

Husband, whether man or woman. This is where we find our purpose in our physical marriages. God teaches a man how to be a husband by living as an example. He teaches us unconditional love, acceptance of flaws, the responsibility of character, and the ultimate role in being the head of our families. Just the same to a woman, God teaches her how to love unconditionally, how to support, how to be a co-manager, yet understand how to step up and be the head manager when needed. He also teaches her the most influential spiritual discipline, submission!

If a man can't love God, he will not be able to truly love his wife, and if a woman cannot submit to God, she will surely not be able to submit to a husband. Understand the woman was already a wife before she was found and the "whoso" was a husband already looking for who will help formulate that these were whole people whose void was full of God before their physical marriage was created.

Wholeness in a Godly marriage starts before the marriage begins. Know that it is always God's will for us to seek Him in the reflection of our marriage. Only through Him will we truly live the lives and the fairytale marriages; furthermore, the question remains, will you be made whole?

8

CONCLUSION

So, we have made it to the end of this small milestone of a journey. I would love to remind those who are now even more excited about marriage that the journey has truly just begun. I want to thank my family and friends for supporting me writing this book. There are way too many names to list but know from the bottom of my heart, thank you!

If I could borrow just a few more minutes of your time to share a bit of my background story to the "why" of this book before we depart our way, it would be greatly appreciated.

My brief introduction at the beginning of this book was very accurate. I dreamed of one day being the best husband and father the world had ever seen. For much of our society's ways, this is normally an attribute and desire of a woman's dream or ambition. However, for me, this was all I ever thought about daily. There were contributing factors, but maybe it was the mere fact that my childhood years consisted of always being around predominately adults, as I was the only child for 13 years before my sibling came.

All I had ever known for that first 13 years of my life was ministry, church, and family. From there, the seed was planted that just maybe this too was my path as well. I found out that Living the dream was much harder than visualizing it. The reason being, I was a late bloomer, and being a big guy, most girls that I encountered either did not find me attractive enough to have me as a boyfriend, or they were too embarrassed to admit their attraction for me. Most of the time, the only thing I gained from liking someone was the label of "big brother." It really felt like my dreams of matrimony would be stifled due to rejections and false standards of women I found to be attractive.

At that time, my view of life caused me to build a false sense of failure toward life, leading me to become empty or void. This feeling continued up into my mid 20's. This is where I decided that it was my time regardless of what God had to say, and I would just settle for whatever came. However, I ran into a beautiful individual who I had previously known years ago from high school. She was my high school crush that I never in my wildest dreams thought I would marry.

The beginning started a bit rocky, and we made it to matrimony, but the marriage itself was short-lived due to things that had not been uprooted and discarded before we decided to wed. Things were harder than they had to be because we didn't take steps to get to know who we were individually and who we were in God; neither did we know what our purpose was for one another. We just knew we were in love and wanted to be married.

Although she and I ended, I'm sure now we probably both can admit that had we not skipped simple yet vital steps; moreover, there may be a huge possibility that things could have worked. Looking back, you'll usually always find that things are never as hard as you once believed. So some advice for you that is reading is that you should keep looking forward, so you never have to find yourself looking back.

After the Divorce, I still felt as though I was again empty and needed to fill the void. I ended up re-marrying within a few years without properly healing and understanding marriage. At that moment, without consulting God fully, I again took on the mantle of a spouse and believed I could handle it. I thought I had learned from my past mistakes; surely I could not make the same mistake…Could I?

The whole process was rushed, and we both found ourselves on the road in the dark with no map or flashlight, trying to make it to the destination of marital bliss. In seeking after the gratification of the title of marriage, I never really took the time to get to know neither of these women for who they were in a friendship nor did I understand their true purposes as my wives.

Both women consequently became casualties of an unpleasant learning experience at their expense. It was an experience that I never intended to learn or cost them. Divorce is sloppy for those who may not know it's disheartening, and the sting of brokenness and the process of separating lasts for what feels like an eternity. Questions seem to go unanswered, blame begins to form, and the hypotheticals are enough to keep you up at night, even after the person is gone and you have moved on.

In all honesty, I didn't want to write this book and felt far from worthy. I even became discouraged mid-way through when I was asked a question one day by an individual when I expressed my intent and the message God had put in my heart to write this book. The question was. "What qualifies you to write a book on how to have a successful marriage, when you have never had a successful marriage, out of two?"

Would you believe that sting of that question buried itself so deep? The knot in my throat and the blank stare in my eyes were evident. I felt in many ways this person had pulled my card, and I was a fraud or a hypocrite writing a book on such. Me! The two-time divorcee that still believed in matrimony! That question stayed and resonated in my mind for a few days. One day as I was walking down the stairs of my parents' home, the Lord's voice came and asked, "Why are you so stressed over that question?" I could not honestly give the reply I knew I wanted to give to God because of my simple embarrassment. Again, God spoke, but this time He said, "Do you not know I have never called the qualified to carry my messages?"

This was said to say that if you're looking for credentials and merits for the best marriage award, I wouldn't have a plaque or ribbon to show. I honestly don't know why God picked me to write and share with you these steps to a beautiful Godly marriage. I don't even know why I have been given another marriage chance. I will convey that my life is to be an example to you that doing something God intended to be done His way, your way; moreover, will never work.

Take your time to see if you match up to God's will for your life concerning marriage. Pray always, and never be afraid to do what God says to do. It will never be anything to hurt you, but definitely to prosper you

(Jeremiah 29:11). I pray that you would take heed from my life and live in the complete wholeness in the abundance of what God has to offer you, and eventually you and your mate. I conclude with this prayer.

"Dear Lord,

Thank You for this opportunity to be used for the glory and the edifying of Your kingdom. I thank You for the man or woman reading this, and I am eternally grateful that leading us to meet, not through coincidence but Your divine coordination. I asked that You would build this individual up to be an example in their own lives as they embark on the journey of marriage. May You never leave their side, and that Your voice always be clear and precise. I ask that You make them whole before seeking after a mate, and when they found or met, their mate would seek You just as much as they do. Through the steps shared in this book, I pray that You would grant them the reward of longevity, faithfulness, togetherness, and, most ***importantly, eternal love for their obedience. God, we understand that marriage represents You in Your entirety, so we just ask that You always be the central focus in this union, which no matter what may come, You will always be the answer or solution. In Your matchless and mighty son's name Jesus Christ, we pray. Amen."***